MOMMY TWINKLE EYES

Letters to my therapist

Glenda L. Hunter

Foreword by
Dr. Beverly A. McMillan

Resource *Publications*

An imprint of *Wipf and Stock Publishers*
199 West 8th Avenue • Eugene OR 97401

Resource *Publications*
an imprint of Wipf and Stock Publishers
199 West 8th Avenue, Suite 3
Eugene, Oregon 97401

Mommy Twinkle Eyes
Letters to My Therapist
By Hunter, Glenda L.
Copyright©2002 Hunter, Glenda L.
ISBN: 1-59244-032-0
Publication date: September, 2002
Previously published by NPP, 2002.

FOREWORD

Mommy Twinkle Eyes is a transparently realistic and beautiful look into the inner life of a small girl of about six years of age-a girl who has suffered almost unimaginable sexual abuse since early infancy. Her letters to her therapist tell us about her struggle of learning to trust this skilled, patient and loving woman as she observes her helping the twenty-something multiple personalities in Big Glenda's psyche find peace and integrate into one whole adult. Mommy Twinkle Eyes makes us cheer as she hugs, encourages and protects this motley crew of alters through their terrible chore of remembering and coming to peace with their abuse.

These letters give us a rare look into the interactions of a good therapist and a patient suffering from child sexual abuse. The fact that it took Little Glenda seven years to come out and be recognized is not so amazing as the fact that she was able to come out at all. Love, hope, and consistency as well as skill were the necessary evokers.

The literature on real-life multiple personality disorder is slim and not always optimistic. This book should be a ray of hope to the patient with MPD who wonders, as Little Glenda did, if wholeness is possible at all (or even worth it). It should be an encouragement to the psychotherapeutic community in their delicate work of rebuilding shattered personalities. Mommy Twinkle Eyes can stand as a role model for them in their oftentimes tedious and difficult work. The lay people who love and live with the victims of abuse have much to learn from this little gem, also. Read it with an open heart.

Beverly A. McMillan, M.D.
Jackson, Mississippi
August 2002

THANKS

There are many people to thank, so to all of you consider yourself thanked. In this little section I really want to thank my family-Steve, Samuel, and Gary. It has been a long road for all of you, and I am more aware everyday of the many things you did for me (maybe that will be another book).

Steve, thank you for hanging in there with me and encouraging me. You always told me I could do it, and many times I just felt like hitting you because I was sure I could not. You proved me wrong; I am better. THANK you for being there to hold me and let me cry on your shoulders many a night.

Samuel and Gary, thank you for being the kind of sons any mom would be proud to have. You never questioned, although there was some wonderment about what was going on with Mom, but you pitched in and helped. You did for me what I could not do for myself. THANK you very much for your part in my wholeness.

My prayer for all three of you is that God will richly bless you beyond your wildest dreams for your faithfulness to the family He has given us.

THANK YOU VERY MUCH

Dedicated to my therapist, one of the most important people in my life. She believed in me when everything pointed to a no win situation. Her consistency showed me that some people do mean what they say. Her firmness showed me you can still care about people even if you have to get after them; hurt does not have to follow correction. Her long-suffering gave me hope that she would never turn on me. Her availability told me she cared. She thought I was a person of worth no matter how fragmented I was and she was willing to work hard for me to be better. She put in long, hard hours helping me reach the place of wholeness. For all of this and much, much, much more, I owe her. I will always consider her an important person in my life.

Dear Lady,

You don't know me but I have a number of friends that come and see you regularly.

You have a very different neighborhood than I am used to; there are big people all over the place. When we first came to your neighborhood, we came with Steve a good friend of ours. He drove us there, and then he talked to this very nice lady. He told her we needed to visit with someone; he told her our problem, and she told him "I know just the person for her to talk to." I was really surprised that she would know someone that would want to talk to my friends and me. She gave Steve your name and made arrangements for us to come to your house.

We stayed in the park while we waited for you to get your house ready for our visit. That was an interesting place; many people came and went all the time. Some of your neighbors talked to us, but we just looked at them and they smiled. We were not used to such a busy place, so we just sat still and whispered to each other; we tried not to move a muscle. We were not sure if your neighbors even liked kids, and we certainly didn't want to cause any trouble.

When you came to the park to get some of my friends, I tried to act like I wasn't even around, but I really kept an eye on everything. I really was looking in the window, yes, I know that is not nice, but I just had to know what was going on. I wanted to make sure everyone was safe. I could not hear all the words that were said, but I could tell no one was going to be hurt.

My friends took turns talking to you; we are all very clever at doing that without anyone knowing. Sometimes it is fun to trick people, but we mostly do it because we are afraid of people.

We have different names for you. They are all good, I like to call you Mommy Twinkle Eyes. I would like to call you this in the rest of my letters. If this is not okay; please let my friends know since I have not come and talked to you yet. I will get the message. You might wonder why I picked the name. Well, when I look into your eyes, I see a little sparkle. As you smile and laugh, they seem to kind of like dance like the stars in the sky dancing around.

I will write more later.

LITTLE

Dear Mommy Twinkle Eyes,

No one said I could not call you this, therefore I officially give you this wonderful title. I'm just so glad.

My friends have been coming to see you for some time now, and sometimes they won't tell me what you talk about. But I have a way of tricking them sometimes, and then some things slip out. They have told me how nice you are to them and how you really listen. Do you know that is not how most big people are; lots of them say you should be seen and not heard. Then if you try to tell them something anyway, they just say, "go play". There are some times little people have important things to say.

It is important for people to listen with their hearts as well as with their ears. Because when children try to talk, the words are hard to find, and they do want some one to believe they have something important to say.

By the way, my friends tell me you are good and can tell them apart already. Keep up the good work and maybe someday soon I will be ready to come and talk to you.

LITTLE

Dear Mommy Twinkle Eyes,

You are an interesting person. You don't seem to have a lot of words like we do, but I have never seen anyone with so many questions.

Every time one of my friends comes and talks to you, the same questions get asked over again:
 1) What's your name?
 2) How old are you?
 3) What do you do? (I think this is the funniest one because some children just hang around and don't do much of anything.)
 4) What do you want to tell me? (You're pretty smart to know that if a person--even if it's a kid--comes to visit, they must have something to say or they wouldn't be coming.)

You listened real good to our answers, and you didn't even write them down, but you remembered most of the time. Your memory is really good, or did someone keep telling you? Sometimes you have a way of being tricky.

I sure like some of the clothes you wear; they are really pretty. Some of us don't like to dress up very much. Pretty dresses don't hide you very well, and most of us like to hide. But the boys don't like them at all, dresses I mean. We all like your blue jeans; they look like what we wear, cause everyone likes blue jeans. Don't they?

Well I guess I just wanted to let you know that I think you have some cool clothes, and I like how well you listen.

LITTLE

Dear Mommy Twinkle Eyes,

We do not like going to the doctor's office. I'm glad Steve could take us. It is always good to have him around because sometimes we're not real sure about people, especially when they are loud. There are sure a lot of loud people in the doctor's waiting room; they don't even seem to care if they bump into you; they just keep right on walking as if little people don't count. I guess they forgot that sometime ago they use to be little also.

It was a pretty scary place. Then I looked up and saw your friendly face. That made me feel better, although I still didn't want to be there; that is one of the reasons I keep going more then coming. Then you looked at us and smiled with your twinkle eyes and said "HI, I'll be right back." When the doctor was ready to see us, there you were smiling, wanting to know if we were okay. I really wanted to talk to you then so I could tell you I really didn't feel okay. The doctor didn't hurt us and just gave us medicine to help us sleep. I can't take the medicine because it makes me sleep forever. Some of the others take it and it doesn't even help them to sleep. I think the doctor needs to give us different medicine instead of all of us the same. Doesn't he know that we are all different? I am sure glad that visit is over.

I hope the rest of your day was good and we didn't take to much of your time, but we appreciate you coming to be with us.

LITTLE

Dear Mommy Twinkle Eyes,

Things have been pretty quiet here these past few days. No one will talk to me about what happened at your house the last time they came to see you. They said if I wanted to know I needed to come, but right now I couldn't come even if I wanted to because the medicine still bothers me.

This morning Amber finally told me about the baby getting scared. Sorry about that. I try to take care of her, but sometimes I just can't. Amber said the men outside your house were really noisy, and she thought they might come in and hurt all of you guys. I think she would have taken care of them; she has been known to beat some people up before. All she could talk about was how she wanted to beat them up. I wanted to cry, poor baby.

Then one of the others told me the rest of the story. She said you went in the yard and told those men to leave and not to come around your house again making such noise. A number of my friends cheered for you. You became a brave hero to them. We have all been taught to be afraid of men. Except for Amber and Bob who fear no one. Also they said that you looked very sad for the sake of the baby; you let them all stay a long time until the baby had quit crying so they could take her home. That was very, very kind of you. Why you would want to take care of the baby like that is beyond me. I am the one that usually takes care of her.

It is very good for my friends to have you to care about them. Do you know that no one really cared about them before? At least not enough to listen to them. I know that they have not said much yet, but we all have to get used to you. You are different than most of the people we are used to being around. Please be patient with us; we are really not that bad.

LITTLE

Dear Mommy Twinkle Eyes,

Hey, it's me again.

I am glad you got a chance to read the story I helped to write- "Little Miss No Name." The little girl who asked me to help her write it has for so long wanted a name, and she thought if she just let you know you could help her. So together we came up with that story. She was kind of disappointed the last time she saw you and you said you had not had the time to read it yet. Then the other day when you said you had read her story, her little heart just jumped with excitement.

Her family is very much like the story, so many children; just like Old Mother Hubbard, she had so many children she didn't know what to do. Her mom had so many children that the little girl seemed to always be in the way. She never felt like her mom knew what to do with her either. You know she didn't really run away; she just wished she could. She was sure no one would miss her if she didn't show up ever again. The saddest part was that she never had a name, and we just always called her little girl. But at the end of the story I asked her what did she want this pretend family to call her after they adopted her. She didn't have to think long before she came up with Cinderella.

Someone told me you had tears in your eyes when you said you read it, and you said it was very sad. The little girl almost left because she thought you were upset with her that she would write such a sad story. But Amber whispered to her and told her to stay and talk to you. Amber might have done that so she wouldn't have to talk to you. They tell me you always want to talk to someone and you're not picky. You did something that surprised them all when she asked if she could be called Cinderella; you said yes. Then she shortened it to Cindy. That was okay with you to. You are the only one who ever cared enough to help her find a name.

Our friend Sally was sure you would never agree to such a crazy thing. Boy was she shocked. She was always known as the princess; now there was Cinderella right in our group of friends. Sally thought it was bad enough that you gave her that name, but now Cindy was even beginning to act special. Even when you heard about Sally, it never decided to change Cindy to something else.

We are not really sure about you yet.

LITTLE

Dear Mommy Twinkle Eyes,

Everyone was talking at the same time today after their visit with you; it must have been a great time. I could not come because the medicine still makes me sleep too much. Some said it was fun, but others said they did not like it, but they all agreed that it was grand for you to share such a special room with them.

First of all, Amber was not very impressed. She thought it was a waste of time, although she did like the part of burying the figure that looked like dad in the sand. I'm sure you know that she is very angry about him hurting us. She would have liked it to be the real thing, but will have to settle for the pretend for now and ever because he is not around for us to really bury. She also liked the knife that was in there, but she was disappointed that it was not real. Sometimes I'm afraid she might hurt herself.

But Cindy really liked the toys. She was afraid to play with them because she hates to get in trouble. Then she found the dollhouse and could not stay away any longer. She told me how she sat and played with the little dolls and you quietly watched, slipping in a question here and there, but she could not really tell me what you asked because all she could think was, "I told the secret;" then she would shake. If she told you the secret, please don't tell anyone, because dad might find us or I guess since he is dead he will just have to have someone else find us. I know he must have told someone to watch in case any of us told. Please forget she said anything. Thanks a bunch.

Someday I hope I will be allowed to come to your special play room. It does sound like fun.

LITTLE

Dear Mommy Twinkle Eyes,

You must have some interesting times visiting with my friends when they come. Sometimes that is all they talk about. I am looking forward to talking to you some day. I hear about very surprising things that happen at your house when they come to visit.

Night Jane has not stopped talking about you. She says that you like her, and you even turned out the lights so they would not hurt her eyes. She is only used to coming around after the lights have gone out. Everyone else is talking about how that amazes them also, the fact that you like her, I mean. I am told she told you the whole story about her younger sister silently crying at night, and she was only trying to help her feel better. We have all been upset with her because we figure she is just like dad and before you know it she will be hurting someone. None of us want that to happen. You took time to let her explain that she really never meant any harm. None of us had listened that long before because we didn't think you could touch someone like that without hurting them, or that there was really no reason to ever do that to anyone else. Even though our big sister did it to us when we was smaller. She must have noticed our silent cries.

Thank you for being so nice in explaining to my friends that Night Jane meant no harm; she was only trying to take care of her sister. I was thrilled to hear that piece of news. Sometimes we can treat our friends not so nice if we don't listen to the whole story. I guess we all need to learn to listen a little better.

LITTLE

Dear Mommy Twinkle Eyes,

Another surprising visit with my friends I am told. Some day I am coming to talk to you. Would you please see if that doctor friend of yours will let me quit taking that medicine? I know he will listen to you. Please explain to him that just because we all live in the same house does not mean we all need the same medicine. It will be good to stop sleeping all the time.

Pat is laughing because he said you looked really surprised when he came in and turned the chair around to sit down. Have you not seen little boys do that before? Sometimes big brothers do that; I guess that is where he got the idea. He said he didn't say much because Susie does most of the talking for them. Did you know they are really good friends? Well they are, and they do most everything together. I don't think Pat even plays with anyone else. He is a very quiet little boy. There are two things different about him: sometimes he thinks he is a girl and he is black. It doesn't seem to matter a whole lot to Susie because she just thinks he's a fine person.

I hear you have also met our friend Red. She is our friend, but some of us are not real sure about her either. She is older then I am, and she is what some people call "boy crazy". I don't understand this liking boys business, but she sure seems to understand enough for all of her friends. She says she'll show us how things work, but seriously most of us could care less. We would just assume she stay away from them as well. But some people are harder to convince then others. Please do us all a favor when she comes and sees you again. Tell her just to not bother with these guys or don't tell us if she does. It is not even a pleasant thing to think about.

We all appreciate your help.

LITTLE

Dear Mommy Twinkle Eyes,

Another trip to the playroom. That has been the talk of all for days. Some have laughed too hard to even tell me what happened, but Amber just keeps storming around not saying very much. I guess something happened with her.

This is the story I got; if it is not right, please let me know. The lady who lives down the street took the others to your house. She is very nice; we visit her often. They got to your house and of course spent time in the playground waiting for the right time to come. When they came into your house, you wanted to know if the children would like to play in the playroom while you and our neighbor talked. They didn't really want to leave, but they try always to obey, so they went in the playroom to play. While you and our neighbor talked, they looked at all the toys, played with the knife, played in the sand, drew on the board, sat at the table drawing, and hid the dolls so no one would hurt them. All the time they were wondering what you were talking about for so long, because you never seemed to have that many words for them; you usually listened, but maybe our friend was doing all the talking.

Finally you and our friend came to the playroom to join them. They didn't ask what you talked about, although everyone wanted to know. They also were trying to be polite. Our friend sat in a chair over by the window, and you sat down with Amber at the little table. No one seems to know just what happened, but they said you and Amber got in a battle to see who was the strongest. I bet that was funny. Although Amber thought it wasn't even worth talking about, the others said it was because you won. Then they thought they might never get to come home because our friend said you had to settle Amber down before she would take them home. Our friend did not seem to think it was funny. Whatever were you fighting about? I hope I never get in a hand fight with you cause I know I am not even as strong as Amber. She is really strong. The others thought it was neat to see someone win with Amber but not hurt her. You fight kind, I hear.

Oh my, I would like to see your playroom.

LITTLE

Dear Mommy Twinkle Eyes,

    I don't really understand why you had my friends put in the hospital. They had been waiting for days, then none of us could tell you good-bye. I thought maybe they had done something to make you mad at us all and you just didn't want us around anymore. It is really hard to understand why all of a sudden we just had to leave. In a strange way we were getting use to coming to your house. Inside myself I cry because I thought you really cared about my friends; then you abandon all of us. Steve says this is really not true, so I will continue to write to you in hope that he is right.

It is harder for me to keep in contact with them. The doctor there has them on some strange medicine. If I go and see them, they want me to take the medicine too; they don't listen to me when I tell them I don't need any. So I don't get to visit with them very much, but when I do they tell interesting things. I'll share them with you because I know that they can't come to your house right now either.

I talked to my friends the other day and they all started talking at the same time, which does sound rude, but this happens because everyone wants to make sure they have a turn. That's when the loudest one wins lots of times. Oh well. I do believe no one is really happy with you except Cindy. Cindy says you are only trying to do what is best for everyone. No one really listens to her because she is too little, and she has been your best buddy since you gave her a name and listened to her untiringly.

There is a lady doctor there who everyone calls Dr. Red because of her red hair. My friends seem to feel toward her like they do you, not really sure. She is very nice but she also asks a lot a questions. Everyone is trying hard to behave, and then maybe they can get home. But the other week Amber got carried away thinking she would hurt herself, and someone told on her. They have all been fighting again; I am glad I was not there for all that stuff. I don't like it when everyone fights. I did see everyone yesterday and peace has been made again. They are even liking Dr. Red.

They must have been talking to Dr. Red about you, because it does seem that everyone is beginning to think you only cared for them, and that is the reason you had them go to the hospital. But you are not winning a popularity contest, sorry. If it makes you feel any better, some days Dr. Red is not either.

But please remember that these friends of mine have never had someone who cares about them. Maybe that will make you feel better when you think they might not like what you did.

When I visit them again I will write and let you know what is going on again.

LITTLE

Dear Mommy Twinkle Eyes,

Hey I hope you have been okay since I have no way of knowing about you right now with the others in the hospital and all. In a strange way I do miss you.

Well I did get a chance to see my friends again. Dr. Red is keeping them there I think forever. Steve does come and see them every weekend. That is the only thing that makes them happy. Now they are getting used to Dr. Red, and she is really not to bad.

The hospital has a number of different things to do. My friends have just been allowed to go to classes; one is crafts and the other is a writing class. The others do not like that stuff too much, so I do try and come to visit at these times. We don't really make anything too cool in the craft class. I have done a lot better than that while I'm at home. Writing is one of my favorite things to do. The teacher in that class just gives us a part of a sentence and we are supposed to write a story. My friends think that is a waste of time, but I rather enjoy it, so I try to do it for them. The teacher does not care which one of us writes, as long as it gets done. She is surprised that I can do it so quickly. I wrote one story about a fly on the wall. It was kind of funny. It was like he was watching the people in the room but no one ever saw him. That is how I feel sometimes.

My friends tell me Dr. Red said they are getting better and they will be able to leave soon. I am really glad. She is talking about them coming back after they leave and do an effigy. It doesn't sound too fun to me, but I'm not even sure what she is meaning. I wish I could call and ask you, because you do seem to know all these things that give us a problem. I do hope it is not something that will hurt anyone. I'm just not really sure if she will hurt someone or not, cause she has said she would hurt our dad if she saw him. My concern is, "will my friends truly be safe?" I will need to come more often if possible to keep a close eye on them.

Well, bye for now. I miss seeing your twinkle eyes. Maybe sometime soon we will be able to come back to your house to visit.

LITTLE

Dear Mommy Twinkle Eyes,

A couple of weeks ago I got the best news in the whole world: my friends got to come home. Sorry I did not write and let you know any sooner, but I was too busy celebrating with them. They were in the hospital a long time. I hope you never have to put them in again.

Yesterday we went back to the hospital to do that effigy I told you about. That was kind of scary at first. When we walked into Dr. Red's office she had this thing made that looked like dad. There were these bib overalls and a plaid shirt stuffed with something that made them look real, and for the head was a balloon with a picture of his face taped on it. I thought it was him. I was out of there. Dr. Red made the others stay. They all took turns looking at it, and no one liked what they saw, but she said they had to stay in the room with it, it would not hurt them. The vote was that she probably didn't know how powerful he was, and she had no idea what he could really do. She being the Doctor, and my friends trying to obey the best they could, they stayed.

Dr. Red had this man put that crazy looking thing in a truck and take it to the back part of the hospital, while the other lady and my friends rode in a van back to that place. When we got there, Dr. Red had this thing already out of the truck and set up. It still looked frightful; I only took a short look. Dr. Red put gasoline on it and then handed my friends matches and told them to light it. The matches went from one person to the next and no one really wanted to do the job. But she kept saying that dad would win if they didn't. I was not sure what he would win, but the others seemed to know so I just watched and listened the rest of the time. I could hardly believe my eyes and ears. First of all, I heard a voice that sounded like my dad saying all kinds of things that he used to say, and the other lady with them said that to make him be quiet they had to light the figure. Cindy turned and asked really nicely if they could please turn it off, and Dr. Red said the only way it could go off was to light the figure. Sometimes good manners don't even help. Anyway, Amber got really mad and said the rest of my friends were wimps and she would light that match. She was kind of happy to do the honors; no one else even considered it an honor.

It began to burn and the tape went off. It almost seemed like magic to me. It just burned and burned and burned until there was nothing left but the wood that held up the figure. The others became more relaxed to the point of knocking over the wood. I was still not sure if they would be hurt, but I did know that I wanted out of there. But it was like I had to finish watching what would happen next. The whole thing was almost gone when the others sat down on the ground nearby and watched. Only ashes left, my friends got up and proceeded to kick the ashes around as they stepped on the wood that lay at their feet. They seemed to really be enjoying themselves. Dr. Red and the other lady were really quiet, and I thought that maybe they had left, but out of the corner of my eye I could see them just standing there watching. No noise was being made, just a quiet understanding; the lack of words was a concern to me. They sat back down on the ground, looked around just a little bit, and one by one they began to leave. I knew they were leaving, and in a quiet way they told me good-bye. I wanted to cry, but I was not sure just how to do that so I did not.

It was kind of a sad day for me. I could not stay really sad because they had come many times to your house to visit in hopes of getting better so they could leave. They had no more jobs to do, and things were looking up for them.

I would like to talk to you about all of this too, but since I still don't come and really talk to you, that would be hard to do. Some day I will come and talk to you. I miss my friends, but thanks to you and Dr. Red for taking care of them and helping them to get well. I hope some day you will help me also, but first I have to trust you enough to tell you all I know.

LITTLE

Dear Mommy Twinkle Eyes,

I know you were really surprised when you were told there were probably other friends of mine that wanted to come and see you.

It looked like you had tears in your eyes. I thought that was kind of scary. What does that really mean? Do you not want to see my other friends, or were you just sad about something else? Tears are hard for me and my friends to understand. We were never allowed to show them to anyone, but many times we had them on the inside. When we had them on the inside, it usually meant that we were hurting or very scared. I hope that is not the case with you. If it is, you can tell us about what makes you hurt, cause we understand hurt. I have seen some people just cry for what seemed no reason at all to me. Maybe some day you can explain all of this crying business to me.

I also heard you say you don't know what to do. I guess you mean you don't know how to help them. Well, you did good with the first group, so please just try. I'm sure it will be okay. I guess the big thing is to listen with your heart and just try to love them, cause you know hardly no one ever showed us too much love. If you have too much trouble, you can always tell them not to come back to your house again and bother you. We have all been told that before; we understand that kind of talk.

I know you said you would see my friends and anyone else who wanted to come and talk to you, but I am still not real sure myself. I guess I will still just watch and listen until I am more sure. My first group of friends said you had good hugs, but I'm not sure I want any of that stuff, hugs sometimes lead to hurt. I guess I will go now. I do believe my friends will be coming to see you soon.

Good Luck

LITTLE

Dear Mommy Twinkle Eyes,

It is a little quieter without my first group of friends around to add their opinion about everything.

I know some of my other friends have come to see you. I even came in your house the other day and pretended to be someone else so you never knew it was me. But I left in a hurry because I know you are hard to fool, and I really didn't want you to know about me yet.

George is quite an interesting fellow to talk to, don't you think? I like the way he can play basketball. When he was younger, he worked hard at being the best basketball player there was. He played other sports, but this was the best. He practiced a lot so he could beat our brother, and that he did. We all cheered for him. We were a little afraid of this brother because he sometimes hurt us. But whenever he tried to hurt George, he would just knock him down or hit him in the stomach. I don't like this very much, but boys will be boys. One has to do what one has to do to keep things in order.

Lilly said she even talked to you the other day when they came to your house. I tell you, she can tell the best stories I have ever heard. She is good about telling the little ones stories. Some are sad and scary but most of them are funny. You should let her tell you one some day. If you are sad, she really can cheer you up.

The others didn't have much to say. I hope you have a good time visiting with my group of friends.

LITTLE

Dear Mommy Twinkle Eyes,

You know the lady that we live with has complained about a headache for days. I hope maybe she will talk to you and you can help her fix it. I know she doesn't come in your house very much either or not for very long, but please see if you can help her.

I think it has to do with Abigail. She reads all the time, and the lady gets a headache. I know that sounds strange, but somehow if Abigail reads without a break it will happen. Maybe it is from her just watching, but it doesn't give me a headache. Abigail cannot even take a very long break between books. She just can't read enough to satisfy her. She does read some good ones, but some are really boring. When she reads the boring ones I just don't listen. I really think that is what the lady should do also. Even when they turn out most of the lights in trying to get her to stop, she just makes her eyes real tiny and keeps on reading. She even gets books with big print so it will be easier to see, cause sometimes she has a problem seeing the words real good. But I guess you know that because she wears glasses. But I can tell you this, that those who do not know how to read enjoy the stories. I might enjoy it more than anyone else because I like the way words sound all put together.

You know what it is about all this reading that I like the most? It is kind of like writing. It is telling a story, and you can really say you never told, because it is different than talking. I really like to write. But sometimes when you write you can say true things, and people just think it is a story. They just don't think you are that sad on the inside, but they really don't take time to talk to you to find out. Some people have read a few poems that I wrote, and they said they sounded sad. Then I quit letting anyone read them. I don't like to make people sad.

By the way, if you have any say in what Abigail reads, ask her to read fun things, or even some children's stories. Some of the ones she reads are hard to understand.

Thanks from all of us.

LITTLE

Dear Mommy Twinkle Eyes,

My friends are not happy with Susie. They have complained for days about the way she acted at your house. Poor Susie just wanted to cry. I did not come, and now I wish I had been looking in the door. I just was not able to make that trip, because sometimes I don't like waiting in the park while you get your house ready. All of the noise bothers me. I know that the noise also bothers Susie, but she really wanted to talk to you.

Some of the others told me about her sitting on the floor with her legs drawn up to her chest and holding them very tightly. I know that must have looked funny, but she is a very scared little girl. I guess you already know that after the other day. She also told you part of the secret; that is kind of scary. Now I guess we have to wait and see if anything bad will happen to us. I know that my first group of friends told you some of the secret and nothing happened, but I'm not sure how long that will last. Fear runs deep.

Did you know that Susie is afraid of water? Well, she is. One time when we were in the creek playing, she splashed water on dad and he got really mad and grabbed her and pushed her head under the water. He didn't let her up for what seemed like forever to her. When she was let go she could hardly breathe. She thought she was going to die. Now she doesn't even like going near the water. We try to keep her away, but sometimes she just finds herself there and she almost panics. I hope she gets over that fear.

She did tell me that she would be coming back to see you. She likes that you don't let anyone bother her while she is there, and that it is okay to cry. Then with a little smile on her small face, she told me that when she got ready to leave you gave her a great big hug. She wanted it to last forever. Then she started to cry cause she had to leave and you told her, "It's going to be all right." That made her insides happy. She says she will get better cause you are going to help her like you did the others.

Please don't let her down.

LITTLE

Dear Mommy Twinkle Eyes,

Something interesting has happened. I think you have met John, or maybe you know him as the preacher. Well, he did a dirty trick on the lady we live with.

She has been working hard at going to school. She studies long hours. It is not easy, because we all make so much noise sometimes she cannot think very well. It is really hard for small children just to sit still and not make any noise. She used to call for us to help her because we all try to help each other; it doesn't always turn out that way, but we try. Well, after studying all by herself for hours, she thought she had the information all wrapped up, but what she didn't know was that John had hidden some of the information from her. She went into that class feeling pretty sure that she would get an A. She took the test and felt pretty good about it, but realized some of the information didn't seem just right. When she got back the test she had gotten a C. She was very disappointed. Boy, was she sad.

A number of days had passed, then you could hear someone laughing, and we all knew it couldn't be her. There was John feeling real good about himself. This is what he told us: "I had that information she needed but she didn't ask, so I kept it hidden." When she heard that, she wished none of us were around. But he said she was getting too cocky and he just was teaching her a lesson.

No one was to tell you, because he was sure you would not be happy. Well, I'm telling because I feel sorry for her. She does try hard. I have been trying to talk someone else into telling you when they come to your house, but I'm not sure if they will. You know we can all be a little stubborn at times.

LITTLE

Dear Mommy Twinkle Eyes,

I am sure glad I can write to you again.

Don't you think Ruth is pretty smart like you? We sure do. But what I don't like is that she doesn't like to teach children. You seem to think children are important, or you wouldn't take all this time talking to my friends that are children. Ruth just thinks big people should be taught. I hope she learns from you that little people need to be taught things also, but not bad things.

I know Clown was not there very long to talk to you, but he doesn't talk a lot. He really likes to make people laugh and laugh. He sure is pretty funny. He kept mom laughing when she was very sad. He can make just about anyone laugh. I don't know how he does it, but when we are sad he can make us laugh also.

I know my friends will not be around long, but I'm glad you got to meet them. I'm not even sure how good they are at good-byes. If they don't come often or tell you good bye, please don't get your feelings hurt. They just are different than some of the others you have talked to.

LITTLE

Dear Mommy Twinkle Eyes,

Do you think you could not have us waiting in the park so long next time we come and see you? It is very noisy, but you do have a nice neighbor who came out and told us you would be ready pretty soon. She is the one that answers your phone and sees if you are home for us to talk to.

I think she saw us walking back and forth on the sidewalk while we were waiting. Since there are so many of us maybe she was a little afraid, but we would never hurt anyone. She spoke very nice to us, and asked if we were doing okay. We told her yes, but that was not the whole truth. My friends sometimes get a little sick when they come and see you, because they are not sure what each other will say, and since they keep secrets, it is a little frightful not to know. No one really wants to lose you as a friend even though you are a different kind of friend than they are to each other. You are still strangely important to them.

I think you are really smart to catch us coming and going so quickly. No one ever noticed or said they noticed before. I was even able to slip in for just a few moments since we were all taking turns. I know I didn't tell you my name, but I didn't stay long. I did stay long enough to see the pictures of your children. That was interesting that you would put their picture up to show everyone, because you do have a lot of people coming to your house. I'm sure you are a good mommy.

LITTLE

Dear Mommy Twinkle Eyes,

I knew the other day that when my friends came they would be telling you they were not coming back. They are not mad or anything, they just are done. I hope you understand, because I'm not sure that I do.

It does seem that after my friends come to your house and visit they start feeling happy, and then they decide to leave. I'm not sure why, or even how it happens. It just seems to be the way things are.

I get sad when this happens, but I know it does seem to be right even if I don't understand. You are a smart women to be able to help my friends. Do you know that the lady we live with tried to get us help before and people didn't know what to do for us? She was very sad. All she ever wanted was for us to be well, and she couldn't find anyone who could help her or us. I'm glad you have helped her and some of my friends get better.

You will be meeting the rest of us soon. Please don't tell the lady there are more of us around, because she doesn't want to really know. We have tried hard to keep quiet as much as possible, but it is getting harder to do all the time. She has heard whispers of us, but she is not sure what is going on. She is tired and needs her rest; she does not get much rest when we come and visit with you.

I will not be writing again until the lady knows that we are around. I hope it is not long, because I do like writing to you. It is like having a pen pal that just doesn't answer your letters, but you hope they read them and find them interesting, and I do understand about you not answering them. You are a busy person and you help a lot of people.

Bye for now.

LITTLE

Dear Mommy Twinkle Eyes,

Hey, it's me again.

My third group of friends have come to see you, and you might wonder when am I coming. I'm not sure. I know this is an interesting group of friends I have. They come and go so fast, but you seem to keep up with them pretty good. Sometimes it is easy for me to come when Alice is in your house, because if I am really careful I can be mistaken for her. I know no one has told you anything about the secret yet, but I do think they will if you just give them a little more time. They are like me- afraid of people. It is very hard to talk to people even when they are nice like you. Sometimes we don't even know what to think of nice people, and we are waiting to see what you want. Everybody usually wants something, even if they don't tell you for a while. We have been waiting for you to tell us what you want, but you never ask anything of us, except for us to come again. If you want something, please tell us soon, cause we sometimes worry about it.

Another thing-when my friends start to tell you their secret, would you please not tell anyone? It is really important that they keep the secret, but if they can't, then it is important that you don't let our family know we told you. You know we could get hurt for telling such information. We have been told big people will not believe us anyway. You seem to believe whatever anyone tells you. I hope we don't disappoint you.

I'm still not sure that we should trust you, but everyone else seems to think it is fine. One day I hope to also.

LITTLE

Dear Mommy Twinkle Eyes,

Christmas is a real cool time of the year all the pretty decorations and bright lights. Then there are all the gifts to buy. Alice enjoys that part the best; it gives her a reason to shop (as if she really needs a reason). She sure spends a lot of money on silly things.

Last year Steve gave her a sleep-and-snore Ernie. It made her laugh and laugh before she even pushed on his hand to make him snore. She even took it to school and shared it with the small children. She would hardly let them touch it; she was afraid they would tear it up.

Now this year Steve gave her a teddy bear, brown and cuddly. She shared that with all of us. She sleeps with it and hugs it so hard she almost pulls out his little arms. The good thing is that she knows how to share. Everyone takes turns sleeping with him.

Steve tries to get everyone something cool. I hope he does cool things for me when he finds out about me. I'm sure he will; he is really special.

I hope you had a good Christmas.

LITTLE

Dear Mommy Twinkle Eyes,

I am sorry that Alice and Day Jane came and told you sad things today. Were those really tears I saw in your eyes? We are not supposed to tell those things to anyone. But now the big secret is out. I think since you are so smart you knew that dad hurt us pretty bad and we are pretty scared of him.

Day Jane usually doesn't have a lot to say, but she sees very good. She saw things even when Alice closed her eyes. When dad pulled out his knife, Alice could hardly stand to look at it, but Day Jane thought someone had to look, so she did. Even when they closed their eyes and didn't want to look, dad slapped them and told them to open their eyes. Alice didn't even look when her eyes were open, but Day Jane did.

The rabbit game (I know that is not the whole name, but I hate what it was really called - skin the rabbit) is a very frightful thing to play; I don't know why anyone would think it was fun. How does anyone think of such a strange game for people to play? We always thought it was bad, but never thought a big person would think it bad because a big person thought of it. Please don't tell anyone. We all hope we can trust you. It is not just you we cannot trust, it is really everyone. But we are trying, cause you always do what you say or you tell us why you cannot.

Alice has bad dreams about that game, and she can hardly sleep. Most of the time she is crying. She holds onto her teddy bear so tight she has almost pulled his arm off. I'm glad Steve gave that to her. He is a good man. He also will hug her when she lets him. Sometimes she doesn't like to be touched by anyone because it hurts, or she is afraid of being hurt.

Thanks for listening to such an awful thing; maybe next time things will not be so bad. We really don't have too many good things to tell you. Sorry.

LITTLE

Dear Mommy Twinkle Eyes,

Some of my friends are not too happy with Susan. They seemed to know that if she told you what she did you would not be happy, and you know no one wants to make you unhappy or mad about what they do.

Now Susan doesn't know what to do. You told her not to take anymore Ex-lax, and now she feels she shouldn't be eating anything. She is very hungry. I tell her to go ahead and eat, just don't tell you about it, but I don't hold as much weight as you do. What do kids know? She thinks I am trying to get her into trouble, but I don't like her being so hungry. When you see her again, will you tell her it is okay to eat?

Alice is still very sad, even though she never talked to you much today. She is afraid and trying to hide. She will be back to see you because she wants to get better. You keep telling everyone they will get better if they just keep talking to you. I'm not sure how that works, but I do see it happen a little at a time.

I know I still have not come and talked to you, but I guess I am more afraid than anyone. I first want to make sure everyone else is fine, then I will take my turn. But I do listen sometimes and see what goes on in your house. I hope you don't mind, but I do feel I need to keep an eye on my friends, cause if anything happens to them I want them out of there quick, so I stay near by.

LITTLE

Dear Mommy Twinkle Eyes,

WOW!!!

I can hardly believe my ears today. There has been great talk going on about my friends' last visit. I am sure this must have happened because too many people told me about it, but I just wanted to see for sure. So if any of this information is not correct, please let me know.

Today after Alice came and talked to you, Bob came to talk. As usual he was not happy. He really spends a lot of time that way, so it is not just you. But he got real angry and had every intention of punching you out. He got up and in your face, and you weren't even afraid of him. You just told him he'd better sit back down, or you would call the security guard and they would take him out of the building. No one could believe anyone would talk to him like that. He was still angry but he sat back down. You told him if that was what he wanted to do, maybe he should leave for that day. He was sure you would not want to see him again. But you said he could come back. But he was not allowed to hit you or even threaten you, or he would have to leave. You are so brave to stand up to him.

He has always thought that sense he is so much bigger than a lot of people, he can just bully them around. But his size doesn't seem to bother you any. I wish I could be that brave. But I don't think that will ever happen. Keep up the good work.

LITTLE

Dear Mommy Twinkle Eyes,

I'm not very happy with you again. Why did you have my friends put in the hospital again? You said it was to keep them safe, but I don't really understand that kind of thinking.

Sorry about how Bob acted when we saw your husband. He stopped by to say, "Hello", just like you said he would, and Bob talked to him. Maybe you would say he yelled at him. He didn't use any manners. You know we have them, right? Well, Bob sometimes forgets to use them. But he was really upset with you. Please tell your husband all of us aren't that mean to people. Next time if he comes and talks to us, maybe Alice can talk to him, cause she has good manners.

I hope they don't have to stay in this hospital very long even though it is nicer than where they were before. But I have problems seeing the others when they are in here because of all the medicine, they give them. Cause when I come they do the same thing as the other hospital and give me the medicine and I can't take all that stuff.

Alice didn't even know they were going there, until she woke up from her nap and there she was. She was real surprised because she was in this room that had only a mattress and pillow. She didn't know what happened. Then Bob told her you had us put in there. Boy, was she sad.

I know that it is because of Bob that they had to go. I heard you tell him he had to go because he wanted to hurt himself. But he is not quick to tell anyone that fact. As soon as I can think straight, because I got some of the medicine today, I will try to tell the others what really happened. If I don't get a chance, will you explain to them what happened so they won't be mad at you? I can tell you are really a friend, or best I can tell, anyway.

LITTLE

Dear Mommy Twinkle Eyes,

I bet you were surprised to see Ann with all her red hair. She is a cute little girl, don't you think? I think her red hair is beautiful. She is trying real hard to get the lady we live with to dye her hair red. I think the lady is getting weaker. Someday when she comes to see you she might be red-headed, so don't be surprised.

It is really bad what happened to Ann. I think it would be awful to be trying to sleep and have some one bother you. Then to be put on the floor to finish your good nights sleep, only to be kicked. I know dad said he didn't mean to, but I think he knew she was there and kicked her on purpose. Sometimes he did things that were not very nice.

Ann doesn't talk very much, but she sure likes listening and being with Alice. They get along pretty good. It is always good when friends get along. I know that you've been told about us fighting sometimes, but we have been trying to do what you told us and talk instead of fight. It sure makes things better in our house. It is not as noisy.

LITTLE

Dear Mommy Twinkle Eyes,

I'm sorry things were so sad in your house the other day. Alice had been wanting to talk to you for days; that is why she kept calling you. She is so sad. It is hard to tell someone bad stuff when you are not sure they will understand, or if you are afraid they will think you are awful, or even be mad at you.

Alice trusts you a lot to tell you about that awful rabbit game. It is the worst game in the whole world. I wish we never had to play it again. Alice even dreams about that game. It did seem to help her to talk to you. I really didn't want her to tell you because I thought you would be upset, and I would never get to visit with you. You sure surprised me. Even after she told you such a game, you still gave her a hug before she left and told her everything was going to be okay. That brought tears to my eyes.

You really do care about us.

I will have to give a little more thought to this, because no one cared about us like that before.

LITTLE

Dear Mommy Twinkle Eyes,

I know you had no choice but to put my friends in the hospital again. Bob sure does cause some trouble sometimes. I know when he thinks about hurting himself he is not trying to get you angry, even though it seems that way. He just feels bad, and he doesn't know what else to do or how else to think. He has always had a problem.

When I was there the other day, I got to see the doctor everyone has been talking about. He is really big. We saw him going down the hall with his arm around a little short guy who works there. Then on his way back to the desk, he stopped and said hi to us. We kind of giggled a little cause it looked a little funny. He wanted to know what was so funny. We didn't tell him we thought he was, cause we even know that's not nice. So we just smiled and he walked away. I think he seems like a nice person.

They have fun things to do in craft time. That is when I like to come. I also enjoy the bingo time. There are two ladies in there; I think they work there, but it does seem like it would be just play. Anyway, they are real friendly. We have started to talk. They wanted to know when I was getting out of the hospital; they didn't understand I was just visiting my friends. So I told them we hoped to get out soon. They say they enjoy having me around. That was good to hear. They didn't even seem to mind that I was not the one who was supposed to be there.

LITTLE

Dear Mommy Twinkle Eyes,

I just got done seeing my friends after not seeing them for a number of days. The news they tell me is that you finally came back to see them. I was real puzzled cause I had begun to believe that you would always be there for them. You do seem not to give up easily. This is the story they told me when I said, "See, I told you she wouldn't stick around."

When you came to the room to visit, things were going along pretty smooth, then Bob blew it. No one seemed to know, and he wasn't telling why, but they said he asked you to bring a knife for him. You got angry, got up out of the chair, and said something about you thought we were making progress but you guess you were wrong. Bob couldn't even stop you. He even walked behind you down the hall, and you acted like you didn't even hear him talking to you. You never even looked back. No one seems to know what made you so angry, but everyone knew who did it. Bob went back to his room and punched the wall, putting a crack in it. He even asked to go to a place Alice calls a time-out room. She said she knew that because she had been there before. The nurses didn't want to let him go, and he told them you even said he could go there. Finally they let him go, but not before they saw the wall. They were not very happy, but they didn't say a lot. Everyone was afraid Bob was going to punch them out. He did go to the time-out room and spent some time beating the bed and wall with a foam bat; then he was fine.

Alice said she was sure Bob had blown it forever, cause they even asked the doctor when were you coming back, and he said "you sure made her mad." He didn't know when or if you would be back. Their hearts sank to their toes. They knew no one would love them again the way you did, cause you were the only person that knew them real good and cared about them anyway. They were also worried cause the doctor wasn't letting them out until you said he could. If you never came to see them again, it would be hard for you to tell the doctor to let them out. But they say you did return and they told Bob he was not to make you angry like that again.

I guess you really do care.

LITTLE

Dear Mommy Twinkle Eyes,

I am glad you let my friends out of the hospital. You do seem to take your time, but I guess you have to make sure that Bob will be okay first.

I thought when I went to visit that it was fun, because I did the crafts. I did a lot of painting. I painted rugs with really cool designs on them. I also played bingo and won a lot of prizes. Some of the others tried to play ping pong, but they had trouble hitting the little ball. I never even tried. Some people tried to talk me into it, but I knew the ball was too little for me to hit.

Well, I am glad I get to come to your house again with the others. I think they will be getting done soon, and then I can come and tell you my sad story.

Thanks again

LITTLE

Dear Mommy Twinkle Eyes,

Alice has been feeling a lot better after talking to you. She still calls, I know, but you never seem to mind. I heard you tell her the last time she came to see you that your neighbor who answers the phone in your neighborhood thought she was your daughter. She thought that was the greatest, cause you know she would like to be your daughter.

Alice has become the life of the party wherever she goes. She has lots of fun with her big friend, Betty. They go out to eat and shop, and they've even been putter golfing. I do think Alice's favorite thing to do is shop. She could look for hours. She likes the fancy things. Not long ago they went to the Disney Store. Alice and Ann decided on a Winnie the Pooh dress. They said it was not the coolest dress in the store, but the coolest one that would fit. They would have much rather had the one with ruffles, but it only came in small sizes.

Sometimes when Alice comes in your house now, I see you smile right away. Your eyes really twinkle when she comes in all ready to tell you the exciting things she and Betty do. Sometimes you spoil the fun by making her work at telling you things she would rather not. Betty says if she tells you what she needs to, they can play afterwards; that is the real reason Alice tells you what happened to her. She really likes to play. Do you know she wasn't allowed to play before?

Alice tells me that if I tell you what makes me sad you could help me. I think I will pretty soon.

LITTLE

Dear Mommy Twinkle Eyes,

I saw how hard you laughed the other day; your eyes twinkled the whole time my friends were there visiting. I guess is was a funny sight. Alice does have a way of tricking people from time to time.

I'm not even real sure I can tell you how Alice and Ann could have pulled off such a trick on Bob. The Winnie the Pooh dress, as they had already told you, was really cool. They just had to wear it and show it off. I guess I don't blame them at all. I like it too. Bob hates the dress and thinks it is really stupid. I guess that is what started them to thinking how can we trick him and get him to let us wear the dress. They told him that you wanted to see the dress, so while he was sleeping they put it on and hurried over to your house before he knew what had happened. Then when he woke up there in front of you, he had this beautiful to some, and not so beautiful to others, dress on. I was watching from the window again, because I just couldn't miss this great event. When he went to cross his legs he could hardly believe his own eyes. 'A dress,' I could hear him say. "Oh those girls!" Then you just couldn't keep the laughter inside any longer. I was afraid he would punch you out because that is kind of how Bob is, but he just sat there frustrated, but not punching anyone out either. The rest of the time even when he tried to tell you something serious, you could hardly keep from laughing. Bob also began to see the humor in the fact that this 200 pounds plus man had a Winnie the Pooh dress on.

I was concerned that Alice and Ann would be in big trouble when they left your house, but Bob never yelled at them. I think you had told him not to, but I didn't think that would matter. I think you are really good for him.

I wonder if I come and talk to you, will you love me as much as you love them? Will you listen to anything I have to say? Will you really be able to help me? If the answer to these questions is yes, I will come some day soon. If the answer is no, please have my friends tell me so I don't come and waste your time. I hope not to hear from you.

LITTLE

Dear Mommy Twinkle Eyes,

I have not heard from you, so I am guessing that you are willing to listen to me also. I will wait until the others have left before I come and talk to you. I guess I just want to make sure everything is going well with them before I really make myself known. I know you probably already know about me, but I do have some things I need to talk to you about.

My friends have been having fun. Bob got to go on a picnic. It was all he wanted to do. Alice of course wanted to do everything, and Ann hangs out with her so, they have done a number of things: shopping, which she has become very good at, putter golf, and one of her most favorites of all-eating out. They are smiling and laughing a lot now, and their sadness seems to have left them. They still remember the sad stuff, but it does not make them cry all the time. It doesn't make them angry all the time.

I guess you would call that getting better. I'm not sure what I call it, but it does sound and feel good to me.

Soon I hope to feel better too.

LITTLE

Dear Mommy Twinkle Eyes,

It was a happy/sad time today. Before my friends came to your house today they were kind of sad because they knew it would be the last time they would see you, but they were sure that is what they should do. Bob was really happy the day had finally come that he could leave, but really deep inside he was also sad. I watched each of them tell you good-bye, and the tears that came to your eyes were a surprise to me. Although I am getting better at figuring a few things out, that is still a little mystery to me. Your big hug helped them to just disappear. I guess it must have been the warmth it had or something; I'm not quite sure. They also cried as they hugged you and left.

Thank you for helping them, but now I am all alone. It is very quiet inside. I guess one kind of gets used to the noise, and it really doesn't sound as bad as some people think it might. I have never been without someone else inside to share things with. Now it is only me and the lady we all had lived with for so long. She does not talk to me as much as they used to. I'm not even sure if she knows I am still around. I hope to come and really talk to you the next time the lady comes and visits you. If you do not want me to come, please just call me and tell me. You can call me at the lady's house if you need to.

Well, I am very sad and not sure what to do now. I guess I will just try to think about the good times my friends and I had.

Good-bye
SAD LITTLE

Dear Mommy Twinkle Eyes,

I did not hear from you, so I guess it was okay to come and visit you. You sure seemed to be a little surprised, but you said it made sense to have a LITTLE around. I'm glad I made sense.

Thank you for talking to me and not telling me to leave. I have never been too sure about you because you just seemed to be too nice. You never yelled at any of us except when someone wanted to hurt themselves. Now even when I come you do not yell; you just want to know why I waited so long to come. One reason is I wanted to be positive that you were okay to trust, but you have not failed yet, so I guess I will take my turn. Then I have some secrets that the others do not, and I wanted to make sure nothing happened to them for telling their secret, so I could come with mine, cause some of mine are really bad. I also wanted to make sure the others got help before you got tired of helping us. They would at least be better, and I can live with what I have if I have to. But we have been coming to your house for a long time now; even your neighbors know our voice when we call you, and you seem to be okay with it all. When we heard about your move, I was sure that was the end of our time together, but you invited us to come to your new house. So I guess you maybe won't mind helping me.

You can still back out if you want. Just call me at the lady's house and I will understand.

LITTLE

Dear Mommy Twinkle Eyes,

Sometime when I come to see you I am really nervous like the others were. I am really surprised that you got so upset when I asked you if I could smoke. It just helps me to relax; the smoke getting in my eyes helps me to not think about what is happening, and I knew I had some hard things to tell. At first I thought maybe you were just upset because I didn't understand what was meant by a smoke-free place. I guess I thought you made the rules for your house, but you said that no one could smoke in the whole place. I know before I came into your house I had to go outside of your park to smoke, but I just didn't understand what the problem was. You do seem to be understanding about most things. I also thought it was funny that you thought I meant candy cigarettes. They don't help as much as the real thing. Then you said the worst thing, that I am to young to smoke. I never thought it mattered how old you were. Dad blew smoke in our faces all the time.

I do want you to know that when I left your house I went to the bathroom in the park and threw all the cigarettes I had away. I hope that makes you a little happy. I just never thought of it being something I shouldn't do. I will try hard to get through this without them. But if I slip, I remember you don't like it at your house and will not ask again.

I hope I don't slip cause I don't want to disappoint you. See you next week.

LITTLE

Dear Mommy Twinkle Eyes,

Now I know why the others had a hard time talking to you. It is not because you are not kind, but it is because the junk we want to talk about is just hard to say. It is hard to tell bad things. I like just to see you laugh and your eyes twinkle, but what I have to tell will not make your eyes twinkle. It will make your eyes fill with tears. I cry on the inside when I think about it.

I know something about the rabbit game that the others did not know, and I really wanted to tell you the other day when I saw you, but I just couldn't bring myself to talk to you. I hope telling you in a letter will make it easier to talk next time I see you. The first time it happened at our new house, my mom watched. I know she was not too happy, but she never stopped it from happening. I have always wondered why. I guess I kind of think it must be because I am just a bad girl, and that is what happens to bad girls. I could see her lips moving, but no words came out of her mouth. I never knew what happened to her words. She always had them before. Do you know what happens to words when they just seem not to be heard? Does the air eat them up?

I am really sad today, because to get better I know I will have to talk to you about all this bad stuff, but I don't know that I am as brave as the others were. Please be patient with me like you have with everyone else, and I will try my hardest not to disappoint you. I will work hard like my friends did, so I can get better also.

Hopefully you can help me now that you know what's on my mind. I hope that will be good enough. But I know that everyone has had to tell their story. I can see that funny little smile you had when my friends asked if it was good enough just for someone else to tell their story. It was a smile that said you were sorry but everyone had to tell their own story.

I am not looking forward to it at all. Just thought I would let you know. See you next week.

Sad LITTLE

Dear Mommy Twinkle Eyes,

Do you know what I like the best about coming to see you? I guess since you are not here to answer, I will tell you anyway. I like the hug, but I already told you that, so I know that's no surprise. But I have never known anyone who has had so many hugs. I was sure you would run out or get tired of hugging people, because I know you hugged my friends every time they came and saw you. I was sure you would not have enough left over for me but you seem to have plenty. Boy, am I glad.

I also like what you tell me about getting better. I know it is nothing new because my friends told me you said the same thing to them. You have told us many things, but the thing that we all have appreciated the most is when you say, "It's going to be all right." You usually say this with a big hug. Sometimes we never believed that, but since you said it, we tried to believe because you never lied to us. Now I think maybe it is going to be all right because the others got better. I am working hard, so maybe I'll get better. I hope so. I really think you think I'm going to get better. I hope I do because I don't want to disappoint you.

You make me feel real special. I like the way that feels. I try to keep that feeling the whole time I am not at your house, but sometimes I don't feel too special because of the things that happened to me. Then I think you will not think I am special when I tell you what happened. I really hope this is not true.
I will see you soon.

LITTLE

Dear Mommy Twinkle Eyes,

Thanks for letting me come and see you the other day. I thought after you got my letter maybe you would change your mind about letting me come.

You make it kind of easy to tell you bad stuff, because you say it was not my fault. I feel real bad deep inside, and I am sure you are wrong about it not being my fault. I am afraid soon you will discover the real truth. I will try to hurry and tell you all I need to, so when you find out the truth that it is my fault, I will be done and it will be too late for you to stop seeing me cause it will be over.

I know what I told you about my mom was really hard to believe, and I was waiting for you to tell me stop lying, but you never did. It really was the truth even though it sounded like a lie. It makes me really sad to think of the whole thing. Dad hurt me really bad, but when mom didn't help I knew there was no use to try and find someone to help. If a mom won't help her little girl, then no one should. That makes me feel like I'm not worth helping. That is why I wait for a call from you, or for you just to tell me to get out and never come again. You have surprised me many times. When my friends started seeing you I told them it would never work. I have been very surprised that you kept your word to them and kept seeing them no matter what they told you or how tired you must have been. You have kept inviting us to your house. Even when you moved to your new house I knew it would be over, but that is where I come now to see you. I still don't quite understand, but I do like how you are, and you give great hugs. I am not used to getting them, but they feel good because I know you don't want anything in exchange for them.

You must be a good mommy to your real children. I hope they see those twinkle eyes of yours.

LITTLE

Dear Mommy Twinkle Eyes,

Well, these past few weeks have been really hard. It is not fun coming to your house when we have to work so hard. I like your new house except for the other time when I came and there was a rat. You seem almost as afraid of them as I do. I worry about you being there. I am glad there is someone there who will take care of things like that for you. I wanted to be brave and help you, but it was all I could do not to jump in your arms. I guess I thought that was being brave for me.

I guess I need to tell you why I am so afraid of them. When I come and see you I hope I can do that, cause right now I don't sleep very well because I dream about them all the time. It is really strange how when I tell you something scary like that, I can stop dreaming about them. I know that is how it was with my friends, but I had hoped I could just stop thinking and it would be okay. But I can't stop thinking. God must like for us to think, or He wouldn't have given us a mind to think with.

My mind seems to be very busy trying to figure out why my friends and I got hurt, but I'm not getting very far. I guess that is one I will never figure out.

LITTLE

Dear Mommy Twinkle Eyes,

Thank you for listening to the story about the rats. I know it must have been hard to hear since you don't like them either, but you listened very good. It must be hard to hear things that make you feel bad too. I think you do a good job of listening with your heart as well as with your ears.

Thanks also for helping me to remember that it is only a memory when I tell you, because sometimes it feels like it is really happening right at that moment. I know it can't be, because you have told me you would never let anything like that happen to me. If you were around when it happened, you would have stopped it. I think you must be really brave and very strong. I wished my mom had been that strong and brave.

You know my dad and uncle did some very bad things to me that made me sick to my stomach. It would make me so sick I could hardly eat for days. I hate when people hurt other people. The preacher at our church says that shouldn't happen. I wish he knew they hurt us, because I think he would try to make them stop. I was just too afraid to tell him. Our pastor is a really good man. He seems to like children a lot. I don't think he even wants anything from them. He just smiles at me, and sometimes he pulls my ponytail. Maybe some day I'll let him hug me like he does the other children. I wish he was my daddy.

Can you adopt a new parent even when you have one of your own?

LITTLE

Dear Mommy Twinkle Eyes,

Thank you for letting me tell you all that other bad stuff. I am really feeling better. I'm not sure how it works that I feel better when I tell you the bad stuff that happened, but it does seem to work.

I think it is about time I leave like my friends did. It is kind of sad, but I do feel a lot better, and I really don't have a job to do any more. You know the lady we stay with is ready for me to leave. I have just had to make sure everything is fine before I go.

I am glad you have been willing to listen to all I have had to say. You know my big friend Betty and I have spent a lot of time going out shopping and going out to eat. That sure is fun. The thing I like to get the best when we shop is socks. I know you have seen most of the beautiful ones I have, but I like the grinch socks the best. They are just the coolest.

I hope the lady I live with keeps all these cools socks even after I leave. Please tell her that would be the thing to do; she will listen to you. Thanks for all your help.

LITTLE

Dear Mommy Twinkle Eyes,

I know you think I am gone, and I did tell you good-bye, but when I heard you were going to have surgery, I just had to stick around to make sure you were okay. You have taken good care of us, and I just wanted to make sure nothing happened to you.

I know you told the lady I live with it would be fine to talk to this man that moved into your old house. I was not sure about him, so I just took it upon myself to stick around until I know everything is okay. I hope this does not make you too mad. Your old house does not look as good as you had it, but I guess it's okay. I talked to him a few times to make sure he is safe for the lady to talk to. I'm not sure he knew it was me. He does seem fine. But I would much rather you not be sick and she could see you forever.

Sometimes I am not sure the lady we all lived with for so long is able to take care of herself. I know she is doing better all the time. But if I am sure you are around in case she needs help, it would make me leaving much easier. I could rest better if I knew she could always count on you like we have been able to do.

I sure hope you'll be back home soon.

LITTLE

Dear Mommy Twinkle Eyes,

You don't know how excited I was to hear your voice on the phone the other day when I called your office. I had the lady we live with call to check on you. I have been counting the weeks for you to get back to work. I talked to Betty and she said you were doing fine. I thought maybe you wouldn't want the lady I stay with to come and see you again after you had time to think about everything we have told you. Maybe you just have gotten tired of all this stuff, cause we sure do. I was very pleased when you set up a time for the lady to come to your house.

I will not be shy about telling you that I did not like the fact that you wanted that man to come to your house at the same time we do. I had hoped I would not have to see him anymore. I don't think he really believes the lady will ever be fully better. That makes me sad to think about, because I am getting tired and want to leave. Will you talk to him and tell him even if he doesn't believe, could he just pretend, because I really want to leave, and I don't know if I should if she is not totally better. She does do most things herself now. I just usually come with her to see that man. It is really important that I feel everything is safe before my leaving.

I can hardly wait to see you again.

LITTLE

Dear Mommy Twinkle Eyes,

When you came to the park while I was waiting to see you, I could have just giggled I was so excited to see you looking cool like always. When you said it would be a few minutes cause you were waiting on the man to come, I tried to let the lady tell you it was okay, but I could hardly sit still. I just wanted to jump up and give you a big hug. Sometimes I don't like how old the lady acts. I guess that's how it is when you grow up.

When we went in a different room of your house because someone else was in the room we usually talk in, I knew you would know it was me. I couldn't help it. Different rooms bother me. I always feel like I have to check them out, make sure they are safe and everything. I know the lady wondered what was going on, cause she felt kind of funny. When I slipped and said something I knew, you knew it was me. I can fool some people, but I can't seem to fool you. You are pretty smart.

I guess I could have cooperated with you a little better, but I thought if I let him talk first maybe he could leave. Sorry for being a little smart alec. I know you were trying to sound like you are mean, but I could tell you thought it was funny. It was good to hear your laugh and see those twinkle eyes even if you were getting after me. The man we saw while you were sick is a pretty good man. I could probably get used to talking to him. He looked like he wasn't too sure what to say. I thought that was pretty funny.

Thank you for not making me feel real bad about being so silly when you were ready for business. Sometimes big people forget little people don't always feel like being serious. When little people are excited like I was, its hard to be too serious. You are a really good sport. So is that kind man. Please let him know I think he is an okay guy.

I am happy/sad right now. I will close and write again (before I completely go) when I don't feel like crying.

LITTLE

Dear Mommy Twinkle Eyes,

I am really leaving, but before I go I do have a few last things I want to say. I know that does not surprise you. I am known for my many words.

I know the lady we have lived with for so many years is able to take care of herself. That has been a real important thing for all of us to know, and the fact that you say she will be okay helps a lot. That helps me to make the move of leaving.

Also, I want to really thank you for hanging in there with me and my many friends who have spent many long hours at your house, some pleasant and many not so pleasant. It never seemed to matter how unpleasant it was; you kept hanging in there with us and telling us it would be okay. Even the times you had to put us in the hospital were done only out of concern for our best. We have never had someone love us so much. I guess maybe that is how God loves.

It is hard to really say good-bye to such a good friend like you. I do hope that sometimes you will see little peeks of us when you see the lady we lived with from time to time.

I do speak for all of us-**THANK YOU VERY MUCH** for all of your help and believing in us when many others have given up and thought we weren't worth saving. You will always be special to us.

Please keep being the way you are, and maybe you will find another little girl that will be proud to call you Mommy Twinkle Eyes.

LOVE

LITTLE

Dear Mommy Twinkle Eyes,

Happy Mother's Day, my dear friend. I have spent my whole lifetime searching for a mommy that would care about me and love me for just who I am. Now that my body has grown to adulthood, I found that someone in you. You have treated us as if we were really precious little ones worth caring about. You gave us strong hugs so many I could not even begin to count. What a wonderful hugger you are. You have cried with us and laughed with us; how interesting it has been to have someone feel for us and with us. You have also gotten after us when we needed correcting, that even has been okay because we know you care.

In the time we have known you, we went from being a frightened, crying baby, to a frightened child, and now to a somewhat uncertain adult. But you have nurtured us into a caring, loving adult. Yes, I owe you a lot, Dear Mommy Twinkle Eyes. Thank you so much for all your caring.

WE ALL LOVE YOU

LITTLE

www.ingramcontent.com/pod-product-compliance
Lightning Source LLC
Chambersburg PA
CBHW051703090426
42736CB00013B/2522